When *Faith* Meets *Promise*

Miracles Take Place

When *Faith* Meets *Promise*

Miracles Take Place

GARY HAWKINS, SR.

HIGHLAND PARK, ILLINOIS

When Faith Meets Promise
by
Gary Hawkins, Sr.

Copyright © 2006 by Gary Hawkins, Sr.

Printed in the United States of America

Published By
Mall Publishing Company
641 Homewood Avenue
Highland Park, IL 60035
877-203-2453

Cover Design by Quiana Clark

Interior Layout and Design by
Faith Instructional Design
551 Mountain Park Trail
Stone Mountain, GA 30087
770-498-6700

ISBN 1-934165-10-7

Unless otherwise noted, all Scripture quotations are taken from the King James Version of the *Holy Bible.*

For licensing or copyright information, please contact:

Gary Hawkins Ministries
P.O. Box 870989
Stone Mountain, GA 30087
Phone: 800-821-6156 Fax: 678-510-1333
vof@voicesfaith.org • www.voicesfaith.org

Dedication

Throughout these past twelve years of pastoring Voices of Faith Ministries, I have met some phenomenal men and women of God who have encouraged me to increase my level of faith to the level of God's promises for me. I have encountered many challenges during this journey, but your example and dedication to the vision of God convinces me daily that I, too, can be blessed beyond my own expectations.

Your many testimonies of God moving simple men and women to greatness constantly reminds me of what God said I am capable of achieving whenever my situation begins to make me forget. Your trust, assurance, and conviction continues to bless and push me to desire greater things from God. I dedicate this book to you.

Acknowledgements

To my God, You are awesome! Thank You for anointing me to be an incredible faith walker. I love You! Thank You for entrusting me with *another* assignment. Thank You for your unwavering grace and mercy shown towards me despite my handicaps. I praise You!

To my lovely queen, Debbie Elaine Hawkins, you are more beautiful every day. You are a breath of fresh air, and I thank God that I have you in my life. Because of you, my world is brighter! You are my greatest cheerleader. When I think I cannot go any further, you push me to go another round. Thank you!

To my four wonderful children—Elaina, Ashley, Gary Jr., and Kalen—I am breathless without you in my life! Your joy and laughter inspires me to live more freely. Thank you for unselfishly sharing me with others.

To my dear mom, Mary Louise Robertson, my love for you is unconditional. I am walking in destiny because of you. Don't stop praying for me and my family. It is working! God is answering your prayers.

To my wonderful mother-in-love, Elzina Owens, your love has caused me to be too blessed to be stressed! I am the most blessed son-in-love in the world.

I wish to especially thank Angia Levels. Favor is now in your house! Now is the time to begin experiencing God's manifestation.

I wish to also thank Ebony Moore for allowing God to use her gifts and talents in this assignment.

Quiana Clark, God has shifted you to a new dimension. Your focus in the kingdom is unbelievable!

To my brother and sister-in-love, Aaron and Mia Hawkins, thank you for ALWAYS being there for my family! I cannot count the number of times we needed you to pull us out of a difficult situation and you did. I love you!

To the rest of my family—Walter, John, Reginald, Denita, Wayne, Aldreamer, Mary, Warren, Victorina, Chris, Theresa, Gladys, Ann, Gail, Shelia, Dwight, Andrea, Michael, Roy, and Judy—God could not have sent a more loving family. Not a day passes by that you are not on my mind. I often pray for your safety as well as prosperity in your life.

To Earl, Jasper, Paula, and Theresa, thank you for accepting me just as I am. I am always praying that God will open windows of heaven and pour out blessings that you cannot contain.

To my nieces, nephews, cousins, and friends (far too many to name), I love you. Thank your for your love and prayers.

To my pastoral staff—Lorraine Dykes, Tyrone Lane, Barbara Jones, James and Valerie Murkison, Althea Brooks, Lakisha Chatman, Neva Romaine, Cynthia Ward, David Ferebee, Dewaine Johnson, Zenda Duren, Laura Walker, Shawnea Barry, Taronda Hall, Bernie Grant, Debra Adams, Dexter Hall, Nikki Washington, Solina Smith, Michael Dupree, Chris Jackson, and Charles Ford—thank you for your commitment and dedication to God's vision for Voices of Faith. Know that you are helping to advance the kingdom. I love each of you beyond measure.

Table of Contents

I need the level of faith that is required for
the level of the blessing.

Introduction

On Tuesday, October 17, 2006, my wife, Debbie and I flew from Atlanta, Georgia to Houston, Texas to "The Church Development Strategies Conference" hosted by Dr. I.V. Hilliard, senior pastor of New Light Church. This was my third year attending. I highly recommend this conference to anyone needing their faith stretched to the next level. The conference is held annually around the third week of October. Its main focus is leadership development. Good leadership makes for a strong infrastructure in any church.

The next day, Dr. Hilliard, who is my mentor and a close friend, invited my wife and me to his home for lunch. This was not our first invitation, but I am always humbled and honored to be invited for fellowship with the Hilliards. Dr. Hilliard's house is the largest house in the state of Texas. Praise the Lord! God has been good to him and his family.

While eating lunch with Dr. Hilliard and Dr. Robert L. Wilks, Jr., senior pastor of Vine-Life Christian Fellowship in Riverside, California, they talked with me about the importance of owning a private jet. Dr. Hilliard owns two jets: a Gulfstream and a Hawker. They said, "The jet is a tool for ministry." A private jet allows you the opportunity to travel to minister the Word of God and gives you the flexibility to return home the same night and be in the comfort of your home with your family. Another perk of owning your own jet is it eliminates the waiting in long lines at the airport. The benefit of flying privately is to save time and minimize wear-and-tear on your body.

Dr. Hilliard explained to Dr. Wilks that he had almost convinced me to purchase a jet, but I was "afraid to pull the trigger." I told him that our church could not afford to purchase a jet because we were in the middle of building our second location in Rockdale County. Dr. Hilliard went on to say, "Gary, the reason you have not purchased the jet is your faith did not **require** the jet. Your faith only **desired** the jet. When you require the jet, God shall give it to you, but as long as you just desire it, you will never have it. When you desire something, it has not processed through your mind, but when you require something, the mind says, 'It is a done deal!' The reason why you are living in the house that God blessed you with is because your faith required the house."

That statement was powerful! Dr. Hilliard taught me that in order to receive God's blessings, I need the level of faith that is required for the level of the blessing.

This book, *When Faith Meets Promise,* will show you how to obtain the level of faith that is required to receive your level of blessing. Many of the promises God has made for your life are left on layaway. This book will show you how to get your blessings off of layaway. It teaches you how to elevate your faith to the level at which God's promises are spoken. You will discover that God will never lower His promises to meet our level of faith, but we must increase our faith to meet His promises. If you closely follow the godly principles in this book, nothing shall be impossible for you and Christ in this age of possibilities.

I pray that your faith will soar to heights never seen before and that you attain the promises of God after exercising your faith through Jesus Christ, Our Lord and Savior. Always remember, when faith meets promise, miracles happen!

When God speaks a promise into your life,
you have to worship Him even when it
seems like the promise isn't coming.

CHAPTER ONE

It Takes Faith

And a certain woman, which had an issue of blood twelve years, And had suffered many things of many physicians, and had spent all that she had, and was nothing bettered, but rather grew worse, When she had heard of Jesus, came in the press behind, and touched his garment. For she said, If I may touch but his clothes, I shall be whole (Mark 5:25–28).

It takes faith to keep chasing something that appears to not want to be caught. It takes faith to keep pursuing something when it looks like it is not going to happen. It takes faith to keep chasing something when God is silent. It takes faith to follow a God who does not answer you. When you wake up every morning and say, "Good morning, God" and He doesn't say good morning back, it takes faith to keep believing the blessing is coming. It takes faith and determination to say, "Look, God, I've been through too much to turn around now. I'm saying 'Good morning' whether You answer me or not. No matter what, I'm still going to praise You today." That's the kind of faith it takes to bring your promise to fruition. It's that kind of faith that still believes God will bless you even when you don't know when the blessing is coming, how it will appear, or who will bring it. It's that kind of faith that still worships God although you don't know when the promise will come to pass. If you are to receive your promise, then you must have the kind of faith that believes God even when it looks like He has run out of blessings.

That's why determination is required. Determination is having a made-up mind. Many Christians do not have made-up minds. They allow people to easily dissuade them from pursuing God's promises. God is looking for saints who have made up their minds to not let anyone talk them out of believing His Word. People who are wishy-washy will go with the latest thing they hear, but when you have a made-up mind, you know what God said and you stand on His Word. You fight to hold on to His Word because you know you are in the right place, and you are doing what God said to do.

I believe that we are in a different season with God. God is looking for true worshippers, people who live a lifestyle of worship. That means that everything in their lives moves them to a place of worship. He's looking for some people who can say, "Lord, I'm not worshiping You to see what I can get from You today. I am worshiping You because You deserve it. Lord, if you don't bless me today, it will not stop me from worshipping You."

God is looking for some people who do not wait to get to church to praise Him. He is looking for people who will wave their hands anytime they feel the Spirit move, even if they are driving, in the shower, or at work. He's looking for the kind of people who will think about His goodness while in the shower and have to put the soap down to shout to the Lord. He wants people who will say, "If I have to go to the bathroom while I'm at work and say, 'God, You are worthy to be praised!' then that is just what I will do."

God is in a different season with us. He knows who shouts based on feelings. He is moving beyond those people who shout, "Hallelujah!" one Sunday and the next Sunday, they say, "I had a bad day. Don't talk to me right now." God doesn't like people who are moody. He wants people who will worship Him when they are going through troubles and when everything is great. If they are happy, they worship Him. If they are sad, they still worship Him. If they don't feel well, they worship Him. If they are sick, they worship their sickness away. A worshipper will praise God at all times.

Once we understand God's desire for worship, we then have to understand victory. Victory does not come at the altar. Victory does not come when you are over-taken by the spirit and lying prostrate on the floor before the altar. Victory does not come when you are speaking in other tongues. God is not impressed with any of that. Victory is in knowing that God has your back every step of the way as you are going through your trials and tribulations. Victory is when you know the battle has already been fought on your behalf. Victory is when you praise God in the midst of your affliction because you know your situation has already been resolved. Victory is being confident that whatever God promised you has already been done, so you can go ahead and praise Him for it now.

Victory also means liberty. Second Corinthians 3:17 says, *"Now the Lord is that Spirit: and where the Spirit of the Lord is, there is liberty."* Liberty means "freedom." It is the opportunity to choose. That means that wherever the Spirit of the Lord is, there is freedom. God gives you the freedom to choose to pursue your destiny. If you don't have your blessing, then you haven't gone after it. If you haven't received your breakthrough, then you haven't gone after it. God wants you to receive all of His promises, but you must choose to pursue them.

Many of us have locked ourselves in bondage instead of pursuing God's promises. Then, we say, "God, I don't understand why my blessing hasn't come." You have the keys to free yourself, but you're still asking God why He hasn't shown up in your life. God has not moved because you are asking Him for the very thing that He has given you the liberty to do on your own.

Your faith meets God's promise when you make up your mind that you will not allow anything to stop or distract you from the blessing that God has promised you. Many of us allow circumstances and situations to distract us and destroy the blessing that God has placed upon our lives. The blessing does not change, but we allow the people around us to shatter our hope of receiving it. You cannot allow this to happen. If you want to receive God's promise, you must have a made-up mind. A person with a made-up mind is unmovable. A person with a made-up mind will not change when the wind changes. A person with a made-up mind says, "I will stand my ground until God shows up. I don't know when that will be, but I have to be where God told me to be whenever He shows up."

When Moses spoke to God, he removed the veil from his face (Exodus 34:34). Moses had an intimate relationship with God. He would talk with Him and fellowship with Him daily. When Jesus died on the cross, rose again, and ascended to Heaven to sit at His Father's right side, the Holy Spirit, our Comforter, came to remove the veil for us. Because the Holy Spirit dwells in us, we are able to talk with God, hear Him speak His promises into our lives, and then walk in whatever He has said.

Galatians 5:1 says, *"Stand fast therefore in the liberty wherewith Christ hath made us free, and be not entangled again with the yoke of bondage."* God has freed us to pursue the kingdom He promised us, and He tells us to not become entangled again with the yoke of bondage. Again? What does He mean by again? God is saying, "I am not going to come and die on the cross for you again, so don't put yourself in slavery to sin all over again! I have already freed you for your destiny. Do not put yourself back into bondage." God did not free you for you to turn around and become a slave again.

Do you find yourself facing some kind of difficulty every week? Does it seem like you are you going through trials and tribulations week after week? The reason you are going through these trials is because the devil knows that God placed something in you. Going through the trials is necessary so God can get the glory when you reach the promise.

When God promises you something, He gives you everything you need to go through the trials to get it. The greater the anointing, the greater the struggle will be. When God has a great blessing for you, there is going to be a great struggle. God will give you the anointing you need to fight the devil at the level of His promise. If your problem seems to be way over your head, know that God has already equipped you with the anointing to handle whatever you are going through. God has equipped you with everything you need to reach your destination.

In our main text for this chapter, Mark 5:25–28, we find a story of a very unique woman. The author of the Book of Mark doesn't even feel it necessary to give her name. He simply refers to her as *"a certain woman."* When you are trying to get your breakthrough, you could care less if the person next to you knows your name. This woman knew who God was and what He could do.

What's interesting about this story is the Scripture is actually talking about a man named Jairus. Jairus was a ruler in the synagogue whose daughter was deathly ill. He had fallen at Jesus' feet and asked Him to come heal his daughter. While Jesus was on the way to heal Jarius' daughter, this woman entered the picture. She wasn't even supposed to be mentioned in this story, but she had great anticipation.

This woman was a worshipper. A worshipper says, "I have to get mine. I can't worry about what other people are doing. I will praise God because He loves people who worship Him in season and out of season. God loves those who worship Him all the time. So, I'm going to worship Him with all my heart." Worshippers know they don't deserve the blessing, but they are confident that God will give it to them anyway.

This woman was minding her own business when she heard that Jesus was coming. She knew what Jesus could do, so she immediately put herself in His path. Worship will move you to the forefront of getting God's attention. Stop thinking, "Well, God knows I'm here. He'll come down my row eventually. He'll come up my aisle sooner or later." I assure you God does not move like that. When you study the people in the New Testament who received miracles from Jesus, they went to where Jesus was. They were people who said, "I really can't afford to wait. He may not come this way again, so I need to make sure I give Him my very best praise while He is here today."

There has to be a sense of urgency about receiving your breakthrough and your promise. You must have the mindset that says, "This may be my only chance to see Jesus. This may be the only chance I have to receive a breakthrough. I can't afford to wait until next week." When there is a sense of urgency, you anticipate God doing something. The woman with an issue of blood knew He may not come her way again, so she positioned herself to touch the hem of his garment. Desperate people do desperate things because they know they can't afford to wait.

This woman had lived in isolation for twelve years. That was twelve years with no friends. Twelve years of shopping by herself. Twelve years of having no one to talk to. The book of Leviticus tells us that when women menstruated, they were considered unclean and whatever they touched was also made unclean. She had been unclean for twelve years. Yet, in the midst of her isolation, she never lost her determination. She spent all of her money going to doctors who did many things; some probably causing her to suffer even more. Yet, she never gave up.

The only way you can really understand her is by knowing how it feels to be desperate. If you have never been desperate for something or someone in your life, then you can't understand what she was feeling. She was so desperate that although she knew she was not supposed to touch anyone, she was willing to step into a crowd of people because her window of opportunity was closing. She said, "I have been suffering for twelve years. I can't afford to wait for Jesus to go to Jairus' house. He may not come back this way. I don't care what anyone says. I have to get my healing."

When you pursue God's promise, sometimes it will seem like you are chasing something that does not want to be caught. That is why you must have faith, a made-up mind, and determination. You must have faith to believe God will fulfill His promise. Then, you must make up your mind and be determined to not let anything or anyone stop you from receiving your blessing.

Many of us never get to the promise of God because our determination falls short. We get weary in our well doing and fall short of receiving God's blessing. We want to get things from God *yesterday* because we don't have the zeal and fortitude to hang in there for a long period of time. That's why we say, "God, if you don't give it to me, I'm going to lose my mind."

You will not lose your mind. God's timing is not your timing. God's thoughts are not your thoughts, and God's ways are not your ways (Isaiah 55:8). When God speaks a promise into your life, you have to worship Him even when it seems like the promise isn't coming. Many of us stop praising God because we do not see the movement of God.

Whenever you are pressing through something, it means there is a resistance somewhere, and whenever there is a resistance, it means that someone is trying to stop you from getting the very thing you are pressing towards. Be thankful for resistance because it builds your faith. If the enemy never pushed against you, you would never strengthen your arms to be able to lift them to worship God. You need resistance because it makes you stronger and wiser. In other words, resistance increases your faith.

This woman demonstrated her faith by touching Jesus' garment, and she received the promise of healing. She had a made-up mind, and she was determined to be made whole. Many of you never get to the touch because you falter in your determination. You falter in having a made-up mind. Just as God gets ready to bless you, you give up.

Let me explain it this way. One day, I was in line at the grocery store. My line was long, and it seemed as if it was not moving. I was impatient. The line next to me was moving swiftly, so I moved to that line. As soon as I got in that line, the lady in front of me had a problem with her check, and we had to wait for the manager to come. I was heated. I looked back at my old line and found that it was now moving quickly while I was stuck in the new line. I wanted to go back to my old line, but I knew I couldn't get my spot back. If I went back to my old line, I would have to go to the back of the line.

Do you keep getting impatient and moving out of your line? Do you have to keep going to the back of your old line? Every time someone else gets blessed are you looking at what they have with envy and jealousy? "They have a new house, a new car, a promotion! Lord, my line's not moving!"

The reality is the grass is not greener on the other side of the fence. You just have to be determined to stand in your line and wait for what is yours. Trust me, what is for you is perfect for you and only you. You don't want someone else's blessing. Just keep pressing. Keep pressing. Keep pressing. Then, watch God acknowledge your faithfulness and blow your mind with what He has in store for you.

God never gives you a vision or promise
that you can access on your own with your
current resources.

CHAPTER TWO

Raising Your Level of Faith

> And when they began to sing and to
> praise, the Lord set ambushments against
> the children of Ammon, Moab, and
> mount Seir, which were come against
> Judah; and they were smitten.
> (2 Chronicles 20:22).

God wants us to raise our faith level to match His promises. Don't be confused when God is silent. It's not that God is unwilling to bless us; it's that we are often unwilling to raise our level of faith in order to receive the blessing. Don't think that God doesn't want you to overcome the obstacles in your life. He wants you to increase your level of faith so that He can bless you. The Word of God tells us that our faith will take us to the promises of God. When *faith* meets *promise*, a breakthrough occurs.

Has God made a promise to you? When He makes a promise, He does not *lower* His standards to meet your current level of faith. It is very important to know that you cannot please God without having faith. Hebrews 11:6 reads:

> But without faith it is impossible to please him: for he that cometh to God must believe that he is, and that he is a rewarder of them that diligently seek him.

That means that if you are going to receive the blessings God has promised, then you must raise your level of faith. When you do, God will honor you at the level of His promise; not merely at the level of your faith. *God never lowers His promise to meet your level of faith.* The reason some of God's promises have not manifested in your life is because you want God to meet you where you are. Because God desires the best for you, He will never come down to where you are. Instead, He will raise you up to where He is. The question we must ask is: Where is God in my life right now?

Here's a news flash: Your whining, crying, bickering and complaining does not move God. That idea messed me up when I first truly understood it. I realized that during those times when I wallowed in depression and sorrow, thinking that God cared about my pitiful state, God was not moved at all. Our emotions do not move God. The only thing that moves God is faith.

Moses pleaded with God on his knees, "God, why are you treating me so miserably? What did I do to deserve the burden of a people like this? I can't carry all these people by myself! The load is too heavy. Please spare me this misery!" (Numbers 11:10–15). God said, "Moses, get up and go summon seventy of the leaders of Israel" (Numbers 11:16). Some people who are reading this right now have been whining and complaining about what they don't have, but God is not emotionally affected by your complaining. If you do not get this revelation right now, thirty years will pass, and you will still be saying, "God I don't understand. Have You forgotten me?" God will not forget you, but He will not move until you meet the standard of promise that He has set. He does not lower His standard for anyone. It does not matter who you are.

Some people will often attend wonderful Christian conferences and revivals to learn how they can grow spiritually and to be delivered from things that are holding them in bondage. Many of these people lie all over the pews and run up and down the aisles begging God for deliverance while others crowd around the altar. As I watched these people over the years, I often wondered why the same people needed deliverance or a breakthrough each year. God showed me that it's because these events are emotional, and we think emotions move God.

You do not need to tell God, "Lord, You know I lost my job. If I hadn't lost my job, I could..." God knows what you went through. He was with you while you were going through it. The challenge of receiving God's promises is in the fact that He will never give you a promise at your current level of faith. When God speaks to you, it is always at an inopportune time, a time when your faith is not ready for that level of promise. He has to stretch you to take you where the glory is. Therefore, God will never speak to you in your time.

If some of you had to give a testimony of what God told you He was going to do in your life, it would blow some folk away. The vision He has given to many of you is so big that the people in your lives would have a hard time believing it, because it is so far from where you are presently. God never gives you a vision or a promise that is on your current level. He never gives you a vision or promise that you can access on your own with your current resources.

God always stretches you to receive whatever blessing He has for you. Your job is to go after it in faith, so that God gets all of the glory. He will never tell you to do something that you can do without Him. He will give you a Word to find out whether you will lean to your own understanding or trust in Him. You will not know how you are going to accomplish it. All you will know is: God said it, and I believe Him.

Two years ago, God told me, "I want you to start a church in Rockdale County on July 18." I thought, "Rockdale County? Lord, I don't know anybody in Rockdale County. And July 18! Why July 18?" I remember thinking, "How random? God, are You giving me specific details?" God specifically said, "July 18."

Once again, God was telling me to do something for which I had no resources and did not feel I had the ability to achieve. Still, I said, "God, I don't have any connections in Rockdale, but I will obey You." I knew I had to move, so I drove around for hours every day in Rockdale County looking for a building. I went to the YMCA. They told me that I had to own land in the county before I could use the YMCA. I was thinking, "I need land in Conyers, Lord." So, then I started driving around Rockdale County every day looking for a building or land.

I went to the Rockdale County Board of Education to ask if I could use one of the schools. They told me that I needed land. I went to a church in Conyers. They told me that I needed land. I said, "I don't have any land!" God just kept telling me, "July 18." I said, "God, I don't know what to do." I went back to the school board, and the school board told me, "We will not allow you to use our facility, if you don't have land in Rockdale County." I needed to be a property owner in Rockdale County before I could use any of the county's facilities.

When God makes a promise to you, He does not give you all of the details. He wants to know whether you will stretch your faith to go get it. A lot of us are waiting on God to come to our level. Here's another news flash: You're going to be waiting forever! I can not stress this enough: God does not come to our level. He does not get glory from it. God is not glorified until He does something in your life that only He can do.

I went back to the Rockdale County School Board. For the third time, the school board told me that they do not allow anyone to use their facilities unless they own land in Rockdale County. Again, I said, "I don't own any land!" I told God, "God, You didn't tell me this was going to happen." I went home and immediately became depressed. I literally made myself sick. I went to bed with a fever, but, in reality, I really wasn't sick at all. It was all in my mind. I let depression consume me. I was in bed feeling sorry for myself. I was bothering my family: "Can you bring me some cookies and milk?" I was lying in bed, and my chest started hurting, or so I thought. Again, it was all in my mind. I began to blame God for my condition. "God, I was fine with my one location. Why did You put me through this?" Do you know what God told me? He said, "Get your butt out of that bed, now! I'm not going to honor another thing you ask of Me until you get out of bed and go!"

"What? Go where?" I asked.

"Go to the Rockdale County. Go to the board meeting, and I'll fight the battle for you," God said.

I attended the school board meeting. When they called my name, "Pastor Hawkins, will you stand?" (This was before I became a bishop.) I stood up, and they said, "You have made an unusual request."

"What do you mean?" I asked.

"We have never had anyone ask to use our schools when they didn't own land in the county, so we're going to table this until the next meeting."

I said, "I have ten days left before I have to be in Rockdale County. Can we table this today?"

They said, "Sir, we haven't even discussed this before. Come back on next Thursday."

I went home and got back in my bed. Your circumstances can mess you up, if you can't see the promise. God said, "Look, I want you to get up right now. Go make some flyers saying you will be in Rockdale County on July 18. Send them around Rockdale County. That's My promise." I had to raise my level of faith to God's level of promise.

In obedience to God, I attended the next board meeting with only three days remaining before Sunday, July 18. One of the board members had one of the flyers in his hand. God told me not to open up my mouth. God said, "All I needed you to do was show up." See sometimes it's not necessary for you to say anything. All you need to do is just get in the right position to receive the blessing. Don't look at your circumstance. Don't entertain thoughts like, "Well, my credit is messed up, so I know I'll never get a loan." God said, "Just show up!" God will say, "Go to the lender's office, and then go to the mortgage company. Just show up."

The board member said, "Pastor Hawkins, didn't we tell you that we were going to table this until next week? Why would you go around passing out flyers in our county telling people that you're going to have church at Rockdale County High School on July 18?" God whispered, "Don't say a word." The board member continued, "How many did you pass out because one of them came to my house?" I said, "I think it was over five thousand." He said, "You passed out five thousand flyers, and you didn't get approval?" God said, "Don't say a word. It is done." The board member said, "This is what we are going to do. Since you wouldn't wait on our instructions, we're going to give you two weeks at Rockdale County High School, and from there, you will be allowed to use Conyers Middle School." Look at what God did! God tested me to see if my level of faith would rise to His level of promise.

You are in a season in which your life should be better. You should be much further in life than where you are today. I just need you to stop reading for a moment and confess this over your life: "I should be living better than I am. I should be living at a higher level." This time repeat it with attitude. "I should be living better than I am! I should be living at a higher level!" Now, begin praising and thanking God for raising your level of faith.

The only reason that you lack anything is because your faith has not yet met God's promise. You want God to come to your level, and God says, "I'm not coming down there." The Lord's blessing is at His level, not ours. Remember, when faith meets promise, something will happen. Something will break when faith meets promise.

> *Then there came some that told Jehoshaphat, saying, There cometh a great multitude against thee from beyond the sea on this side Syria; and, behold, they be*

*in Hazazon-tamar, which is En-gedi. And
Jehoshaphat feared, and set himself to seek
the LORD, and proclaimed a fast throughout all Judah (2 Chronicles 20:2–3).*

After hearing of a great threat, Jehoshaphat sought
the Lord. It is good to have a threat every now and then.
You need to know that you are only one threat away from
your breakthrough. You don't even understand how
close you are. You are about to give up on life. You're
about to give up on that business, and you are only one
threat away from your wealthy place. You are one threat
away from going into millionaire status. Think of it this
way, if you are never threatened, you will never get on
your knees and pray, "God, they are threatening me!"

Your enemies need to be careful when they threaten a
child of God; especially, when you fully understand
whose you are and who you are in the body of Christ.
People on your job should not threaten you because God
will use that threat to set you up for a breakthrough. In
fact, the enemy would be better off just leaving the children of God alone because his threat only forces you to
call on your Father, who has all power.

In the midst of the prayer, King Jehoshaphat gath-
ered all the people together, and in his prayer, began to
remind God that He was God. Of all the people in the
crowd that God could have chosen, He chose to speak
through a member of the choir by the name of Jahaziel
(2 Chronicles 20:14). There were preachers and deacons
in the building. There were gatekeepers and greeters in

the building too. I asked God, "God, why did you speak to Jahaziel? You didn't bother to speak to the preacher. Why did you choose a member of the choir?" God said, "I wanted to speak to someone who would sing and praise when I spoke a Word. I wanted to speak to somebody who did not look at Me like I had lost my mind when I sent a rhema Word." So God spoke to Jahaziel because He was used to worshipping and praising God. Jahaziel stood up and yelled, "Hey everybody, I just heard from God! Start shouting right now because God is about to do an astonishingly awesome thing."

> And he said, Hearken ye, all Judah, and ye inhabitants of Jerusalem, and thou king Jehoshaphat, Thus saith the LORD unto you, Be not afraid nor dismayed by reason of this great multitude; for the battle is not yours, but God's. Tomorrow go ye down against them: behold, they come up by the cliff of Ziz; and ye shall find them at the end of the brook, before the wilderness of Jeruel. Ye shall not need to fight in this battle: set yourselves, stand ye still, and see the salvation of the LORD with you, O Judah and Jerusalem: fear not, nor be dismayed; tomorrow go out against them: for the LORD will be with you
> (2 Chronicles 20:15–17).

That was the promise! According to Galatians 3:14: "That the blessing of Abraham might come on the

Gentiles through Jesus Christ; that we might receive the promise of the Spirit through faith. " It is impossible for me to receive any promise of God without operating in faith. We have not manifested more in our lives because when God makes a promise to us, we think it is over our heads. It *is* over our heads! It is supposed to be over your head so God can get the glory, not man.

When God tells you to go to the mortgage company and apply for the loan, believe Him for the loan. God knows you are not working; however, He also knows that this is the breakthrough you need to start your own business. You have to trust that God knows what He is doing. In the natural, we become afraid when God speaks to us and what He says appears to be too big, but we must believe and act in the spiritual.

How many people do you know, including yourself, to whom God showed a vision or spoke a Word regarding what you were going to become? The vision or Word was so big that you could not see or know how it could come to pass at your current state of mind and level of faith. Out of excitement, you shared this Word with your family and friends only to have them place doubt in your spirit. You didn't know they would be dream killers. Now, your vision is a threat.

If someone says, "You know God didn't speak that to you," you should get excited because when people start saying what God didn't say, it will force you into praise and worship. You will stay on your knees a little longer until the breakthrough occurs. While waiting, God will do one of two things: He will either fight on your behalf or He will let you fight for Him. Sometimes God will tell you to just stand there, and sometimes God will tell you to go to battle. You may get a few bumps and bruises along the way, but in the end you will be victorious. Don't let what you see discourage you from acting on what God says.

Before completing our first building, God told me, "You shall build a building on this property." At that time, we only had thirty members, and fifteen of them were children. By the time we moved into the building in 1999, we had seventy-five members. Seven years later, we have over nine thousand members, and have built or acquired over seven buildings. Each year, God blesses us with another building. I didn't let the fact that I had a small congregation discourage me from believing what God said. God doesn't want you to ask Him how. He only wants you to believe Him. Your job is to get in the right position to receive the manifestation.

Can you imagine one million soldiers with guns, spears and swords ready to attack you, and God says, "Don't fight. Just show up"? Don't be discouraged by what you see. Instead, stay encouraged by what God says. God has revealed to me three "Ps" that are necessary for you to receive His promises:

1. **Position:** *Get yourself in the right position to receive the promise.* Many people believe God for a new career, but never send out a resume.

2. **Posture:** *You don't need to fight just stand.* When you get to the place of promise, act like you are supposed to be there. In other words, walk with a confidence, which demonstrates the assurance of your belief in the promise.

3. **Perception:** *See the salvation of the Lord.* People should be able to see that there is something different about you. You may have fallen on bad times, but you are still a righteous person. You are still a child of the King, and you have a right to the promises of God.

Our problem is that we want a microwave blessing. We want to testify without having gone through the struggle. The struggle is the necessary process. We don't want to go through what we have to go through in order to receive the blessing. We want to give a testimony of victory without showing up for the battle.

When faith meets promises miracles take place. If you sit at home and do nothing, your situation will not change. In the process of getting in the right position, you may experience rejection. One door may close, but two or three will open in its place. Know that you have a right to the very thing that you are asking God to do, as long as it is according to His Word.

You need to develop a King Jehoshaphat spirit. He consulted with the people only to reassure them that they didn't have to fight. He told them to praise God for what He had done and what He was getting ready to do.

There are some things in your life that you have been trying to battle on your own, but God is saying that it is His fight. Quit trying to do it yourself. You can't do it yourself. God has to do it. God has to manifest it. God has to bring it to pass. The enemy is preparing his weapons and sharpening spears. In other words, the enemy is still lying on you and talking about you. The enemy is setting up ambushes to try to defeat you, God's Word says:

> No weapon that is formed against thee shall prosper; and every tongue that shall rise against thee in judgment thou shalt condemn. This is the heritage of the servants of the LORD, and their righteousness is of me, saith the LORD"
> (Isaiah 54:17).

Understand that the weapon may form, but it will not prosper. Moses got in position, had the right posture and the right perception, and through his obedience, God parted the Red Sea. That same God will fight the battles in your life.

King Jehoshaphat reminded the people that God caused manna to fall from heaven six days a week. He also reminded them of God's miracle at the Jordan River, when the priests placed their feet in the water and the river split. Jehoshaphat asked, "What about David killing ten thousand Philistines alone? And don't forget Sampson killed thousands with a jawbone of an ass!"

King Jehoshaphat was only reminding the people that He is a God who is faithful and they needed to trust Him. You have to trust God sooner or later. Why not now? I know you feel out numbered, but God's Word tells us that *"Ye are of God, little children, and have overcome them: because greater is he that is in you, than he that is in the world" (1 John 4:4).*

I have heard testimonies from members whose houses were about to be sold on the steps of the courthouse when one telephone call was made on their behalf, and the sale stopped immediately. We cannot run from our battles. If so, we will continue fighting the same ones until we learn to overcome them.

King Jehoshaphat appointed singers and placed them on the front line. But when the singing started, God didn't move. The people in the church were shouting, but God didn't move. Even when the people started speaking in tongues, God still did not move. Have you ever experienced that? Have you been praying, crying, shouting, and speaking in tongues only to have God still not move? That's because God was not impressed. God will not move until you move.

Have you stopped to check your level of faith? You can't drive a car without checking the oil and changing it regularly. When you don't check your faith level, often, you may be operating on old faith and don't know it. We say things like, "Lord, I'm just going to wait on You. I'm not going to move until You move, God," while God is saying, "I'm not going to move until you move."

I'm reminded of the four lepers in 2 Kings 7. These lepers were at the gate talking. They said, "If we stay here, we're going to die, and if we go back to Jerusalem, we're surely going to die. If we go back to the enemies camp, we may die, but we may also live" (2 Kings 7:4). After much discussion, the lepers rose at twilight to go into the enemies' camp. God caused the enemies to hear a noise of chariots as if there were a million soldiers marching toward them. The Syrians thought that it was a full army. There were only four lepers walking toward them, but the whole Syrian army fled, leaving all of their food, money and treasures as they ran for their lives. The moment the lepers decided to make a change, was the same moment in which God honored their faith and began to move.

The ten leper men who stood outside of the gate telling Jesus to heal them is another case of God moving because someone put their faith into action. Jesus instructed them to go see the priest. As long as they stood in front of Jesus, nothing happened, but as soon as they started walking away, their leprosy began to disappear (Luke 17:11–14). The reason that you are not seeing a manifestation of God's promises in your life is because you are not moving in faith. You pray for a house and believe God is going to bless you with one, but you never go house hunting. You believe God is going to bless you with a new car, but you haven't gone to test drive a car. You have to do more than believe; you have to act on your faith. Remember, God will never give you anything unless you operate in faith. Keep Galatians 3:14 in mind: *"That we might receive the promise of the Spirit through faith."* If you never move, God will never move.

When reading the Bible, always take note of the word *and.* This word is the bridge that connects your faith to the promise. There has to be an "and" in your life for God to move. You will know you have made the connection when you hear yourself say, "...and when I heard the Word of God..."

After you get the "and," then comes the word *when.* Second Chronicles 20: 22 says, *"And when they began to sing and to praise, the LORD set ambushments."* It was not their praise that caused God to move. God moved because they trusted His promise.

Praise is two-fold: It lets God know that you are going to move in faith on what He said, and it is a warning signal to the adversary. Whenever God speaks a Word to you and you begin to praise Him, it ricochets in two directions. Your praise summons Heaven and tells God you are in agreement with Him and that you believe what He said. It then summons hell to confuse the devil because he can't understand why you are moving when your current situation looks defeated. So God just sits and waits to see if you will move on His promise.

Have you discovered that God has more time than you? The devil's job is to make you think you have all the time in the world. We call that a spirit of procrastination. That's the spirit that says, "I'll do it tomorrow" or "I'll go to church next week." Time is not your friend; it is your enemy. You cannot put off until tomorrow what you need to do today.

I can't count how many times I have heard people say, "By this time next year, I'll be debt free." Those same people never stop spending. They use all types of excuses to keep from committing. Those excuses are actually causing them to live below their means.

You can live better than you are right now, but you cannot receive a Word from God and just sit on it. The grave is full of people who had great ideas. The man or woman who had the cure to cancer left this world searching for a solution because he or she procrastinated. When God speaks to you, you have to believe what He says and move on it.

How do you increase you faith? The Word of God says, *"So then faith cometh by hearing, and hearing by the word of God" (Romans 10:17).* The more Word I get in me, the greater my faith becomes, and the stronger I become. The more Word I receive, the greater my worship will be and the greater my praise will be. The more Word I know, the greater my assurance that God will deliver on His promise, so I can pursue what He has for me.

On the other hand, if I have little Word, I have little faith. The less Word I have, the less worship and praise I have. The less Word I have, the poorer my attitude will be because I won't believe His promises. But if I have great Word, I have great worship and I'll act like a fool when God speaks to me because I know what God is about to do in my life.

John 10:10 reads:

> *The thief cometh not, but for to steal, and
> to kill, and to destroy: I am come that they
> might have life, and that they might have it
> more abundantly.*

God is telling you it is time to give Him control of
your life. I know you are asking the question, "But how
do I just give God control?" You have to increase your
faith so that God may exercise His promises. Romans
4:17 says, *"Calleth those things which be not as though
they were."* Every day you have to kill your flesh and
speak positively into your spirit. Every day you have to
encourage yourself that you can do it. If God is going to
bless anyone, why shouldn't it be you? He's given you
promises to pursue, but you have to act like they have
already come to fruition. Don't be afraid of the cost.
God will make a way for you to receive His blessings
when you go after them.

Now, some people will come against you just because
you are God's elite. Whenever you are a worshipper, you
are considered God's elite. Second Chronicles 20:23 says:

> *For the children of Ammon and Moab
> stood up against the inhabitants of mount
> Seir, utterly to slay and destroy them: and
> when they had made an end of the inhabi-
> tants of Seir, every one helped to destroy
> another.*

The Bible says that the very people who came against Jehoshaphat began to argue and fight amongst themselves. They began killing each other. God told Israel, "All I need you to do is get to the right position and just watch the glory of God."

And when Jehoshaphat and his people came to take away the spoil of them, they found among them in abundance both riches with the dead bodies, and precious jewels, which they stripped off for themselves, more than they could carry away: and they were three days in gathering of the spoil, it was so much"
(2 Chronicles 20:25).

In other words, when they got to the place of promise, everyone who was against them was dead. Earlier, I stated that you are one threat away from your breakthrough. By the time you find the house, God will bless you with the finances to walk into your dream home. By the time you select the car, God will place blinders on the person who pulled your credit. In a matter of twenty-four hours, the children of Israel went from being broke to being wealthy.

Always remember, you must have faith to receive God's blessings. The promises of God are only received by faith. You must believe you have a right to receive the blessings. Many people don't believe they have a right to receive God's blessings. You have to believe that you are to be a lender and not a borrower. You have to believe that you are supposed to be living better than what you are now.

I declare this Word on your life right now! Some things are about to shift in your life, but you have to believe that you have a right to receive it. You have to believe that God will manifest it. You have to believe that when your faith meets God's promise, miracles will happen in your life.

As you read this, I am declaring and decreeing that the next time you hear God speak into your life, regardless of how crazy it may sound or how farfetched it appears, you will begin praising God for it. You will shout to let God know that you are in agreement with Him and you believe in faith that He is going to do it, even though you don't know how. The how is not your concern. Your only concern is to believe God for the blessing and get in the right position with the right posture and perception.

I am not moved by what I see.
I am not moved by what others say.
I am only moved by the Word of God.

CHAPTER THREE

Accept the Promise

Hearken; Behold, there went out a sower to sow: And it came to pass, as he sowed, some fell by the way side, and the fowls of the air came and devoured it up. And some fell on stony ground, where it had not much earth; and immediately it sprang up, because it had no depth of earth: But when the sun was up, it was scorched; and because it had no root, it withered away. And some fell among thorns, and the thorns grew up, and choked it, and it yielded no fruit. And other fell on good ground, and did yield fruit that sprang up and increased; and brought forth, some thirty, and some sixty, and some an hundred (Mark 4:3–8).

Whenever Jesus taught a parable, it always had a two-fold purpose: to teach His followers about the Kingdom of God and to confuse the enemy. Usually, He had to explain the parable to His disciples to help them understand exactly what they meant. In this chapter, we will look at the Parable of the Farmer Scattering Seed. I will try to explain it in such a way that it deepens your understanding of what happens when faith meets promise and enables you to confuse the enemy.

Jesus explained that the parable shows what happens when people hear the Word of God. He described four types of hearers. Here is what He said about **the first group** of hearers:

> *The sower soweth the word. And these are they by the way side, where the word is sown; but **when they have heard, Satan cometh immediately, and taketh away the word** that was sown in their hearts.*
> *(Mark 4:14).*

Jesus said that as soon as some hear the Word, Satan comes and immediately snatches the Word from their hearts. They hear God's Word, but refuse to obey it, and therefore do not profit from it. Ninety percent of the church body is this way. We hear the Word, but we refuse to profit from what we have heard. That's why we think there is something wrong with people who actually profit from God's Word. They look abnormal because the normal people hear the Word for years, but never profit from what they have heard.

Jesus was actually telling us why some of us have not receiving our full blessings from God. It is not because we have not heard the Word; it is because we listen, but do not obey what God said, so we cannot profit from what we heard. In other words, we do not truly understand what we are hearing. We are in the church, but the church is not in us. We leave the church fired up and ready to do God's will, but some time between the benediction and Monday morning, Satan takes the Word from us because he knows what the Word will do if we ever let it saturate into our spirit.

The devils' job is to keep the Word from really getting into your spirit. Have you ever eaten something that tasted good when it was freshly cooked and when you reheated the leftovers on the next day, it tasted even better? That's because the seasonings had settled into the food. The devil's job is to stop the seasoning of the Word of God from settling into your spirit. He knows that if it settles into your spirit, he cannot stop the blessings that God has ordained for you.

Satan snatches God's Word from you by causing you to forget what you heard God say. That's why you are not profiting from the Word of God. It is time for manifestation. It is time for you to break through the barriers that Satan has created to prevent God's Word from getting into your spirit.

In his attempt to wipe you out, the first thing Satan does is take the Word from you so that you will not have a foundation upon which to stand against him. When he takes away your foundation, you will always revert back to what you know instead of what God told you. John 10:10 says, *"The thief cometh not, but for to steal, and to kill, and to destroy: I am come that they might have life, and that they might have it more abundantly."* Satan knows that if the Word gets into your spirit, you will not only have life, but have it in all the fullness that God intended.

In Mark 4:16, Jesus described **a second group** of hearers: *"And these are they likewise which are sown on stony ground; who, **when they have heard the word, immediately receive it with gladness.**"* Have you ever noticed people who hear the Word and immediately start shouting, "Oh my God, that's my Word!"? They shout because they receive the Word with gladness. They are excited. When they hear the word, they think, "I knew I was supposed to come to church today because that Word was just for me." They are fired up! Then after receiving the Word with gladness, they encounter the issues of life. After shouting and crying about what they just heard, life happens. Because of the "stuff" in their lives, their hearts become hard and they forget the promises of God.

If you are in this group, you need to understand that the promise stays the same, but the circumstances of life are messing up how you perceive the promise. You may wonder, "Why doesn't my faith meet the promise?" If you don't have the Word in you, then how can your faith meet what God says? You can't just be excited about the Word, you must know that when God gives you a Word, the devil will try to take it from you. Satan knows that if you keep that Word in you, then you will receive everything God has promised you. That's why you have to confess it in order to possess it. That's why you have to speak it in order to receive it. Speaking God's Word stops the devil from being able to block your blessings.

Jesus continued describing this type of hearer in Mark 4:17 saying:

> *And have no root in themselves, and so endure but for a time: afterward,* **when affliction or persecution ariseth for the word's sake, immediately they are offended.**

The person who receives the Word with gladness cannot endure persecution, trials, and tribulation alone. After you get the Word, you are glad and excited. You assume there will not be any persecution in your life now that you have Jesus. You think that now that you have the Word, all of the promises will be manifested immediately. What you didn't know was Satan was also sitting in church. He heard the Word as well. He heard what God told you. So when you left church, he went with you. Remember, Satan's job is to take that Word from you; to kill, steal, and destroy. If he can't just snatch it from you, then he will take you through trials and tribulations.

The devil saw you dancing with the choir and heard you shouting about how you're going to get your inheri-

WHEN FAITH MEETS PROMISE

tance. So he brings "stuff" into your life and suddenly
you're offended. You tell God, "God, I don't understand.
I have been in church every day this month, Lord. Every
time they had something I was there. I was tired Lord,
but I still went. Why are you doing me like this, God? I
have been faithful. I have been tithing. I have been
obedient. I serve in every capacity of the church. Why do
I have to go through this, Lord?" You are offended
because you believe you are exempt from trouble because
of your faithfulness in church. You are offended because
you shouted on the Word! The devil got to you by using
troubles to kill your excitement. He had to take that
Word from you because if he hadn't, you would have
gotten too serious about pursuing the promises of God.

Do you remember when Satan told God, "Of course
Job fears You. If You remove Your hedge of protection
from around him, he will curse you to your face"? (See
Job 1:9–11.) That's what the enemy does. He sees who is
worshiping God, and then he brings troubles into their
lives because they are getting too serious about the Word.

Satan is setting you up for failure, but God is setting
you up for a blessing. After you receive the Word, Satan
tests you by whispering to you, "What is taking so long
for God to fulfill His promise? Why is all this stuff
happening in your life?"

When you receive the Word, you have to protect it
immediately. Once you hear the Word, you have to hold
on to it tightly and not let it go until you reach the destiny
God has promised you. The devil will try to take God's

Word away from you the whole time you are pursuing God's promise. He doesn't want you to receive your blessing, so he sends trials and tribulations. However, you must know that the testing of trials and tribulations will not kill you. The only reason God even allows trials and tribulations is to find out if you will trust what His Word says or what the enemy is telling you.

I recently saw a sign on the wall of a restaurant that read, "Don't tell God how big your problem is; tell your problem how big your God is." God really wants to find out what is really controlling your life: the problem or the promise? You have to find out who is really in control of your life. You must look at yourself and ask which of these people in the parable am I? Am I the one who hears the Word of God, but the devil has taken it from me before I can get to Bible study on Wednesday night? Or am I the one who shouts after I hear the Word, but loses it when the devil brings trials and tribulations into my marriage, into the lives of my children, on my job, into my finances, or into any area of my life that means a lot to me. Which type of hearer am I?

In Mark 4:18–19, Jesus described **a third group** of hearers:

> *And these are they which are sown among thorns; such as hear the word, And* **the cares of this world, and the deceitfulness of riches, and the lusts of other things entering in, choke the word, and it becometh unfruitful.**

WHEN FAITH MEETS PROMISE

These hearers are materialistic. They feel like they must have a certain kind of lifestyle. They are so focused on pleasing themselves and impressing others that they forget what God said. God wants you to have a wonderful life, but you are focusing on the lifestyle first, and then seeking God. The Bible says, *"But seek ye first the kingdom of God, and his righteousness; and all these things shall be added unto you" (Matthew 6:33).*

This is what chokes the Word. After hearing the Word, we are inspired to do kingdom work. When we do the work, we start getting blessed by the Word. When you were seeking God, you made it to church, but now your business is prospering and you can't make it to church anymore. After hearing the Word, your marriage gets much better, so you don't come to worship service anymore. After hearing the Word, God blesses you with a new vehicle and a better house that is a little further from the church, so now it's too far to drive to get to church. When you didn't have a car, you used to catch a ride to church. You would call friends and ask, "Can you swing by and pick me up?" You even made deals: "I'll get someone to take me home, if you can just get me there." Now that God's blessings are flowing into your life, God is on the back burner, and you become unfruitful.

When you are unfruitful, God cannot use you. Unfruitful people are in church, but nothing is burning inside of them. You look like a Christian, but you are really a zombie. You are not making a difference in the lives of others because the world has messed you up.

Jesus describes **the fourth group** of hearers in Mark 4:20. He says: *"And these are they which are sown on good ground; such as hear the word, and receive it, and bring forth fruit, some thirtyfold, some sixty, and some an hundred."* These people withstood Satan's attacks. They found a way to survive. They knew the attack was coming and braced themselves for it. They knew Satan was going to send his hurricane so they prepared. How do you prepare for a hurricane? First, you board up the windows. Then you store supplies that you will need such as food, water, flashlights and batteries. You brace yourself for the storm.

These people hear the Word, receive the Word and produce fruit. Their hearts are good ground, so the Word is deeply rooted. There are three things you must do to be in this group. First, **you must hear the Word.** God commands His people to hear Him over 150 times in the Bible. Whenever you read, "Hear Me!" in the Bible, God is trying to get your attention. This means that it is very critical that you listen to what He is saying.

Ninety percent of the people in the body of Christ never move pass hearing the Word. Why do you think people can't tell you on Wednesday night what was preached on Sunday? On Monday, you will hear some of them exclaiming, "My God, we had church on Sunday!" But if you ask, "What was the sermon about?" Nearly ninety percent of them will not remember. "Oh, well, ummm…I know he said something about Jesus!" Satan has already snatched that Word from them.

The second thing that is required to be in this fourth group of hearers is: **you must accept the Word.** This is the main battleground man faces. This is your battlefield. Satan doesn't have to stop you from coming to church. His goal is to stop God's Word from taking root in your heart. You have to fight to keep the Word. God will not allow Satan to stop you from hearing it. However, He will give Satan permission to try to take it from you after you have heard it. Remember, Satan said, "I can't get to Job because you have a hedge of protection around him. Let me get to him and take away all the things he holds precious. Let me bring affliction upon him. Let me create havoc in his marriage. Let me have his wife to tell him to just curse God and die. Let me get to him, God!" Notice, God gave Satan permission to attack Job. In fact, God brought Job to Satan's attention by asking:

> *Hast thou considered my servant Job, that there is none like him in the earth, a perfect and an upright man, one that feareth God, and escheweth evil? (Job 1:8).*

God will allow Satan to come in and try to take the Word from your after you have received it. The battle starts immediately after the benediction. Satan may even send someone to attack you before you even leave the sanctuary. You may have to rebuke the person who was sitting next to you right after you hear the Word. Your battleground is not a physical place. It is a spiritual and mental place, and you must be ready to do spiritual battle. Ephesians 6:12 says:

> For we wrestle not against flesh and blood, but against principalities, against powers, against the rulers of the darkness of this world, against spiritual wickedness in high places.

The third thing that you must do to be in this fourth group of hearers is to **produce fruit.** The Word says that if you accept the Word, you shall be fruitful. It does not say "might" or "may." It says you *shall* produce fruit, if you accept the Word. The key is: You must accept the Word. The only reason your faith will meet the promise is because you accept God's Word. Once you accept God's Word, you shall produce fruit!

You receive a paycheck because you work to earn it. You cannot just show up on pay day expecting a check when you haven't worked prior to pay day. You may get upset and demand, "Where is my money?" But you won't get a check because you did nothing to earn any wages.

That's how some of you treat God. You didn't accept His Word and then you get upset because no fruit is produced in your life. That's why you say things like, "I'm leaving the church! That's it! God is not real!" God is real. He's just not real in your life at the moment because you are not serious about Him.

Jesus is telling us that each of us is represented by one of the people in this parable. If we are not seeing God's promises manifested in our lives, then the Word is either falling by the wayside and being snatched away, or the trials and tribulations of life are withering it so that it doesn't become deeply rooted in our hearts.

When you receive the Word, you have to hold on tightly to what God gave you. Even when you fall, you will still have the Word. You may get bruised, but you cannot let go of the Word. The devil's job is to stop you from going where God is taking you. It is critical that you understand these things in order to receive the promise. You must have faith. Remember, *"Faith cometh by hearing, and hearing by the word of God" (Romans 10:17).* I have to hear the Word in order to have faith. The devil says, "I'll never allow you to get the Word because if I let you get the Word, then you'll have faith, and your faith will get you to the promise. That is why I take the Word from you before you can get it into your spirit."

This is why you can always find a seat at Wednesday night worship or Bible study. The devil knows he does not have to worry about folk as much on Sunday morning. The Wednesday night crowd is who he has to be concerned with because they are the ones who are really serious about the Word. Serious worshippers know that God's Word will increase their faith and their faith will get them to their promise. That is why Satan messes with you after you have had a long day at work on Wednesday. He knows that you're serious about getting the Word, and the Word increases your faith. Your faith brings your promise to fruition.

There is an old saying, "If God said it, that settles it." Whether you accept it or not, God's Word is final. It doesn't have to be settled into your spirit to be true. Just the fact that God said it is enough to settle it. Isaiah 55:11 says:

> *So shall my word be that goeth forth out of my mouth: it shall not return unto me void, but it shall accomplish that which I please, and it shall prosper in the thing whereto I sent it.*

So if God made a promise to you, it will come to pass, *if* you accept it! You must produce fruit when you accept God's Word because His Word will not return to Him void. God's Word will accomplish whatever it is sent to do. But it will not produce anything in your life until you accept it.

Luke 8:15 says, *"But that on the good ground are they, which in an honest and good heart, having heard the word, keep it, and bring forth fruit with patience."* You must have *patience.* You must know that after you have done the right things—heard the word and accepted it—your fruit is coming. This is the process: God will send a promise first. The promise will be beyond your current level of faith. It will get you excited when you hear it, but you may encounter a problem right after you hear it. That's so God can see if you will focus on the promise or the problem. If you focus on the problem, you will be like ninety percent of Christians who never receive the promise. I pray that after reading this chapter, you will join that ten percent of those who hear the Word, accept it, and bear fruit with patience. Don't let what you see discourage you from believing what God said. Speak to your issues and say, "I'm not moved by what I see or what others say. I am only moved by the Word of God!"

Whatever you are looking forward to
God doing in your life, you must
tell someone first.

CHAPTER FOUR

Confess the Promise

And the LORD said unto Gideon, By the three hundred men that lapped will I save you, and deliver the Midianites into thine hand: and let all the other people go every man unto his place (Judges 7:7).

Mark Hankins, author of Spirit of Faith, says, "God is like an air traffic controller. He sees incoming faith, the location and the movement of faith. When your faith is in action, it shows up on God's radar screen, and He releases His power to you." Mark is saying that the moment that you begin to move in faith, God sees you on His radar. If you are not operating in faith, God does not act because faith is the one thing that pleases Him. I believe that God rewards those who diligently seek Him.

In this chapter, I will share Scripture that teaches us that we must confess the promise, believe it and increase our current level of faith in order to reach God's level of blessing. Jeremiah 1:12 says that after God casts the vision, He becomes a watchman over the promise. He watches over the very promise that He made to you to make sure His plans are carried out. Getting your faith to the necessary level to receive the promise depends on you. God doesn't sit over you to make you increase your faith, so you have to find a way to get to where He is operating. God is not going to lower His level of promise to where you are.

Many Christians never receive their full blessings from God because they are waiting for God to spoon feed them. People want God to speak the promise, and then come down to Earth, and hand it to them. They want God to do the whole thing for them, but God does not operate that way.

If you are going to go to the place that God has spoken into your life, then you must use the weapons God gave you. The first weapon is your *mouth.* Unfortunately, most Christians keep what God has revealed to us to ourselves. We will not tell others what God has said because we are afraid of being embarrassed if it doesn't happen. We think if we don't tell anyone what God has promised us, then we won't look bad, stupid, or ignorant. Most of all, we do not want to look like we don't have a relationship with God, if the promise is not manifested in the time and way others expect.

However, I want you to know that if you don't tell someone what God is about to do, you will never see the revelation. If you are ever going to get to the level where God is trying to take you, you have to open your mouth and let the people around you know that God is getting ready to bless you.

Second Corinthians 4:13 reads:

> We having the same spirit of faith, according as it is written, I believed, and therefore have I spoken; we also believe, and therefore speak.

Notice that *"spoken"* is in past tense. Paul said that God spoke a Word to him, and he believed it. He had to tell somebody! The moment that God speaks to you, and you receive a Word, you should tell someone what you just received from God; regardless of what they think. You must be delivered from anyone who is hindering you from receiving your blessings. This includes family members, friends, or acquaintances—anyone who is stopping your blessings. How are they stopping your blessings? You won't tell them what God told you because it sounds crazy. Your faith is not on a level where you are bold enough to speak of God's promise, so God is not moving.

Speak the things you have heard from God. When you finish reading this chapter, tell someone, "If you don't watch me closely, you will miss what God does in my life, and you will have to ask someone what happened!" Declare, "My situation has changed!"

You must confess it before you possess it. Whatever you are looking forward to God doing in your life, you must tell someone first. You have to tell someone, "You are looking at a miracle!" You have to tell someone, "You are looking at a multi-millionaire. You're looking at a lender and not a borrower. You're looking at someone who is in the front and not the back. You are looking at someone who is blessed in the city and blessed in the field. I am blessed coming and going." You have to tell someone! In order for Voices of Faith to acquire each of the buildings that we own, I had to stand before the congregation and confess it.

Too many of us allow the devil to talk "trash" to us while we just sit there and take it. God gives you the ability to talk back to the devil. The devil will tell you things like:

- "You know you are not qualified for that job."
- "You don't make enough income to qualify for that house."
- "That is not your mate."
- "Your children won't be anything."

If you never say anything back, you will start believing his lies.

The woman with the issue of blood had this condition for twelve years before she spoke to her problem. She said, *"If I may but touch his garment, I shall be whole" (Matthew 9:21).* She said this aloud. Even Jacob spoke aloud when he wrestled with the Lord saying, *"I will not let thee go, except thou bless me" (Genesis 32:26).*

I fully understand that I cannot be silent. I have to speak back to the enemy. When someone attempts to speak negative thoughts into my spirit, I stop the enemy in his tracks. Before he gets started good, I tell him, "Satan, I'm going to stop you right there before you can say something that I might not like."

If I believe that God is watching over my promise, then I have to be willing to fight to bring it to fruition. I must fight to get to where my promise is. I must pursue it. I must take authority over it. I cannot be wimpy, soft or lazy. I cannot be laid back.

I played basketball when I was growing up, but I did not play in an organized league. I grew up playing basketball on the streets. If you have ever played basketball on the streets, then you know that street ball players will talk you out of your own game by telling you what they are going to do to you. They say things like, "I'm going to cross you over with my right hand. I'm going to throw it back over with my left hand. I'm going to right base line, and then I'm going to throw it in your face while I'm looking at you!" After hearing all of this, when you get the ball, you will not be able to shoot, pass dribble or rebound. As a matter of fact, you will not be able to score at all. When you go for a lay-up, they will hit you and knock you down. Then, they will talk about you while you are down. "I told you not to bring that weak mess up in here!"

That's what the devil does to you every day. But we have to stand up and say, "Is that all you got, Devil? Was that your best?"

David was just bringing sandwiches to his brothers when he heard Goliath talking trash (1 Samuel 17). When David faced Goliath, Goliath looked at David with disdain and said, *"Come to me, and I will give thy flesh unto the fowls of the air, and to the beasts of the field" (1 Samuel 17:44).* Goliath was talking noise saying, "I'm going to take your flesh and give it to the birds of the air and the beasts of the fields." But David cut him off. Here's what David said to Goliath:

> *Then said David to the Philistine, Thou comest to me with a sword, and with a spear, and with a shield: but I come to thee in the name of the LORD of hosts, the God of the armies of Israel, whom thou hast defied. This day will the LORD deliver thee into mine hand; and I will smite thee, and take thine head from thee; and I will give the carcases of the host of the Philistines this day unto the fowls of the air, and to the wild beasts of the earth; that all the earth may know that there is a God in Israel. And all this assembly shall know that the LORD saveth not with sword and spear: for the battle is the LORD'S, and he will give you into our hands (1 Samuel 17:45–47).*

David basically said, "Goliath, let me tell you what I'm getting ready to do to you!" You have to shut up the enemy by talking back to him. Talking back to the devil will increase your faith. The more you talk, the more your faith increases. You have to tell the devil, "I am not fooling with you today, Satan. You can't even be around me today because I'm going to sing about God's goodness all day. I'm going to wave my hands and stomp my feet. I'm going to bless the Lord with my soul and all that is within me. I am going to bless His holy name. You've got to go, Satan, because the Lord inhabits my praise, so you can't do nothing but flee!"

When you start talking back to the devil, your faith will begin increasing to reach the level of God's promise. Revelations 19:21 says, *"And the remnant were slain with the sword of him that sat upon the horse, which sword proceeded out of his mouth."* The man who was riding the horse, looked amongst the enemy (the remnant) and said, "All of you are dead," and they were destroyed.

In Judges 7, God decided to use Gideon, who was considered a coward, to save Israel from the Midianites. Gideon was hiding in a wine press. The Midianites had 135,000 soldiers. The Israelites had 32,000, and God said that that was too many. He said to reduce them to 300. Remember, God will always send you a promise that is over your head. How can 300 men beat 135,000? In the natural, it sounds foolish, but God uses the foolish things of the world to astonish us. That's why when God promises you something that seems crazy, you can feel assured that it is absolutely God at work in your life. He will never give you something that you can do by yourself.

> *And it was so, when Gideon heard the telling of the dream, and the interpretation thereof, that he worshipped, and returned into the host of Israel, and said, Arise; for the LORD hath delivered into your hand the host of Midian (Judges 7:15).*

Worship is another form of rest. I worship because I believe what God said. So it becomes a form of rest for me. Notice *"delivered"* is in past tense. Gideon divided the three hundred men into three companies and put trumpets in their hands. The trumpet was a ram's horn. He also gave every man an empty pitcher and placed a lamp within the pitcher. The ram's horn was to signify that the battle had already been fought and won. They did not have to fight.

The same is true for you. You don't have to fight on your own behalf. You just need to increase your faith to the same level of God's promise. Each man had a trumpet in one hand and an empty pitcher with a lamp inside in the other hand. They brought no swords to the battle. God put one hundred men on the east side of the camp, one hundred on the west side, and one hundred on the north side. Gideon told them:

> *When I blow with a trumpet, I and all that are with me, then blow ye the trumpets also on every side of all the camp, and say,*

The sword of the LORD, and of Gideon (Judges 7:18).

They had to blow the trumpet, break the pitcher, and then say, *"The sword of the Lord and of Gideon."* Notice, God did not act on the promise until they confessed it. You have to open your mouth and say what God has promised.

After they blew the trumpets, broke the pitcher, and said, *"The sword of the LORD and of Gideon,"* the three hundred Israelites watched as the Midianites fought each other. Judges 7:21 says, *"And they stood every man in his place round about the camp; and all the host ran, and cried, and fled."* They met the criteria of the promise. It was God's job to do the rest.

After reading this, I pray that none of you will continue living in lack. If you do, then know that you are the only reason that you have not received God's promise. The only reason that you have yet to experience God is because God will not do His job until you do yours. God is still waiting for you to come to the level of His promise.

The Lord wants to bless you. Some people in the church don't believe Numbers 23:19, which says, *"God is not a man, that he should lie; neither the son of man, that he should repent."* He does not contradict His own Word. Second Corinthians 4:13 says, *"We also believe, and therefore speak."* I worship God; therefore, I confess. I praise God; therefore, I wait on the manifestation of His promises.

WHEN FAITH MEETS PROMISE

Ask God to confirm what He said to you. Romans 10:9 says:

> *That if thou shalt confess with thy mouth
> the Lord Jesus, and shalt believe in thine
> heart that God hath raised him from the
> dead, thou shalt be saved.*

In order to get into the Kingdom of Heaven, you have to confess with your mouth that Jesus is Lord. So there must be something in confession that God wants to hear in order for you to possess what you are speaking. Let me put it a different way. Romans 4:17 says, *"Calleth those things which be not as though they were."* You have to speak something, even though it doesn't exist right now, as though it does exist. You must speak it! Any promise God makes to you that is on a higher level than your current level of faith must be spoken before it will be manifested.

If you trust God for what you have learned in this chapter, then thank Him right now. Tell Him how much He is blessing you. Tell Him that you think He is marvelous. Bless the Lord with your mouth. Confess your promise by saying, "God, in the name of Jesus, I receive what You promised me. I will walk in faith. I will walk with assurance and confidence like it's already done. I will talk like it's done. I will no longer be shy about telling anyone what You are about to do in my life. If the enemy tries to quench Your Spirit in me, I will use the weapon you have given me. I will open my mouth and speak the Word of God."

God never forgets His Word. The problem
is that the issues of life have made you
forget what God told you.

CHAPTER FIVE

The Window of Promise Is Still Open

And when Jesus was entered into Capernaum, there came unto him a centurion, beseeching him, and saying, Lord, my servant lieth at home sick of the palsy, grievously tormented. And Jesus saith unto him, I will come and heal him. The centurion answered and said, Lord I am not worthy that thou shouldest come under my roof: but speak the word only, and my servant shall be healed (Matthew 8:5–8).

The centurion in this Scripture was an officer in the Roman army who was in charge of one hundred soldiers. Everything about the centurion should have prevented him from receiving God's blessing. First, he was a Gentile. The Jews believed God's blessings were reserved only for them. Secondly, he was a man of war.

Jesus was a man of peace. So, why did this gentile, an officer in the Roman army receive a blessing from God?

He received his blessing because he understood authority. The Centurion was used to taking orders. He was also used to giving orders. The Bible says that he was a man under authority. In other words, he was subject to the authority of some one over him, so he was accustomed to taking orders without questioning the authority of the person giving the orders. He was also given authority by those above him; authority that was to be respected by those under him.

When you enter the U. S. military, you are no longer your own property. You are considered property of the United States. That means that you have to dress like your fellow soldiers, get up when they get up, and do what they do. If you buck the system, you can be thrown into jail and dishonorably discharged.

Many of us have been in the church all of our lives and will not take orders from God. The reason why many of you are still waiting to receive your blessing is because you will not take orders.

The word *beseeching* means "to cry or plead." This man who was under authority and in authority beseeched Jesus to heal his servant who was sick of the palsy. Now remember, the Centurion was not a member of the church. He didn't go to worship. He didn't go to Bible Study or Sunday school. He never went to BTU (Baptist Training Union). Yet, he understood how to worship God.

Verse six of the text says, *"And saying, Lord."* Notice that Lord is capitalized. That means he recognized that Jesus' authority was greater than his authority. If he thought Jesus was under his authority the Scripture would have used a lowercase "lord." The Centurion continues saying, *"...my servant lieth at home sick of the palsy, grievously tormented" (Matthew 8:6).* His servant was paralyzed and about to die. So Jesus told him: *"I will come and heal him" (Matthew 8:7).*

Remember, God's promise will always exceed your current level of faith. Hebrews 4:1 (NIV) says, *"Therefore, since the promise of entering his rest still stands, let us be careful that none of you be found to have fallen short of it."* I thought that I had missed my opportunity to be blessed, until I read that verse. This verse tells us that the window is still open for you to receive the promise that God made to you. God says it's still open!

Because of His great love for you, God is showing you mercy. He is giving you a chance to stop looking at your circumstances. Here's an example of this principle in action. God tells you, "In six months, you are going to be debt free." Suddenly, life hits you and things go out of your control. You get another credit card and take out another loan in order to pay your debt. You have taken your eyes off of the promise. You are looking at your current situation and have forgotten what God promised you. When you start thinking that God has forgotten about the promise, you start working in the circumstance.

WHEN FAITH MEETS PROMISE

God never forgets His Word. The problem is that the issues of life have made you forget what God told you. God does not change! But your issues will trick you into thinking He has changed. Just because you haven't seen it yet, doesn't mean that it will not be manifested. God wants to know if you are going to look at your circumstance or trust Him, the One who made the promise.

Hebrews 4:2 says, *"For unto us was the gospel preached as well as unto them."* You have heard the Word preached, but it did not profit you. Why did the Word not profit you? Because it was not being mixed with faith! The only reason you haven't received the manifestation of God's promise is because you haven't exercised your faith. The Word of God says it's not because you haven't been preached to; it's because you're not combining your faith with the Word!

Here is another example to help you understand what this means. As a child, I used to watch my mother make a pitcher of Kool-Aid. Mama would first fill the pitcher up with water. I would ask, "Mama, what are you doing with all of that water?"

"I'm making Kool-Aid," she would say.

"But Kool-Aid isn't that color."

"Yeah, but I got the ingredients in this packet of the Kool-Aid. I have to mix it in the water, and then add some sugar and stir it together. Then you get the flavor that you want." Mama made the best Kool-Aid!

I now understand that when I take the living water, which is Jesus Christ, the living Word, and add an ingredient called faith to it, I will get the flavor that I desire! That means you are right where you are according to your faith. You are allowing yourself to be where you are because of your level of faith. Your level of faith is why you are living the way you are living. Everything that you have right now is because of the level of faith you have in the Word you receive from God. If you are not where you desire to be, it's because you told God, "Stop! This is all I can handle."

Hebrews 4:3 says, *"For we which have believed do enter into rest."* What is rest? Rest is God's holding tank for people who are waiting on the manifestation of His promises. Those who *hear* the Word and *believe* mix their faith with what they hear God say. The moment you mix your faith with the Word, God puts you in His holding tank. He calls you into a place of rest and all you have to do is shout until the manifestation of your promise.

> *For we which have believed do enter into rest, as he said, As I have sworn in my wrath, if they shall enter into my rest: although the works were finished from the foundation of the world (Hebrews 4:3).*

Everything you can ever desire was already finished before God ever made the world. If you can think of it right now, it was finished before God formed the earth. God said, "If you can believe the Word, then your promise is already done." All you have to do is get into a place of rest and shout.

Praise God while you are waiting for the manifestation of His promises in your life. The promises are already complete. God just hasn't brought them into the realm of the Earth where you can see them tangibly. Your house is already finished! You already have the promotion! You just have to wait for the manifestation.

When you finish reading this book, you should take authority over everything that is going on in your life because God has given you the authority to do so. He has given you the authority to take back your husband, your home, and your environment! Take it back! You just have to exercise your faith.

Let's return to the Centurion man in Matthew 8. Remember, in order to receive the promise, you have to raise your level of faith to where the Word is so you can see a miracle performed.

> *Jesus saith unto him, I will come and heal him. The centurion answered and said, Lord I am not worthy that thou shouldest come under my roof: but speak the word only, and my servant shall be healed"* *(Matthew 8:7–8).*

In other words, the centurion told Jesus to just speak the *promise* and he would believe his servant would be healed. He didn't need to wait until he got home or to discuss it with anyone. He said, "Jesus, if you speak it right now, I'll believe it right now!" The centurion explained, "I am under authority. When I tell people to do something, they do it. But I am not worthy for you to go to my home, Lord. I'm messed up. But if you only speak the Word, Lord, that is all I need. Lord, I will receive the Word as soon as you speak it."

Have you ever seen in Scripture where Jesus was shocked? God is omnipresent. He is everywhere at the same time. He is omnipotent, which means He has all power. And He is omniscient, which means He has all knowledge in His hand. How can you shock a God who already knows what's going to happen before it happens? Yet, in Matthew 8:10 it says, *"When Jesus heard it, he marveled."* How can you shock a God that already knows? He marveled! Your faith has to be ridiculously extreme for God to say, "Oh my, who is this?"

Jesus marveled and said, *"Verily, verily I say unto you, I have not found so great faith, no, not in Israel"* *(Matthew 8:10).* Jesus was saying, "I've not found this kind of faith in any of my churches."

How do you get faith? *"So then faith cometh by hearing, and hearing by the word of God" (Romans 10:17).* Since he had not been to church, from where did the centurion get his faith? He was trained to respect authority. He was taught that when a word is spoken, it does not require a question. You hear it, and you move.

"And Jesus said unto the centurion, Go thy way" *(Matthew 8:13).* The word *"Go"* is capitalized. It represents authority. *"Go"* is the promise. Initially, Jesus promised, *"I'll come and heal him" (Matthew 8:7).* The centurion stopped that promise when he said, "No, you

don't have to come to my home." He forced God to make another promise because of his ridiculous faith. Because of his faith, he said, "Just speak the word. You do not have to come." So Jesus spoke with authority, *"Go"* *(Matthew 8:13).*

Now, the question is: Was his servant healed when Jesus said, *"Go"?* No. Even though Christ had all power in His hand, the servant was not immediately healed when Jesus said, *"Go."* Do you know why? What activates the promise? When God makes a command, you must move. If you do not move, then His Word is still just a promise. Jesus said, *"Go"* with all of the power that was within Him, but the centurion had to move for the promise to be manifested.

You need to understand that *"Go"* did not mean, "Go get him and bring him back to me." *"Go"* does not mean, "Stop at your mama's house on your way home for her to pray with you first." It does not mean you need to consecrate something. *"Go"* means "go." That word is only powerful in the life of the believer.

Jesus told the centurion, *"Go thy way; and as thou hast believed, so be it done unto thee" (Matthew 8:13).* This is the first time in the Bible where Jesus said *"believed"* with a "d." Jesus didn't normally talk like that because before this story of the centurion, people's faith was not at that level.

The Scripture says that the servant was healed in the same hour. When was the servant healed? He was healed when the Centurion *went.* Let's look at it this way: Will you become a millionaire because I said it? No, you will become a millionaire because God spoke it through me for you *and* you have to exercise your faith for it to be manifested.

God says that your window of promise is still open. Isn't that worth praising God? In my messed up behavior and with my messed up mind, all of God's promises are still available to me. Even with my messed up ways, He still has enough mercy to hold onto my promises until I can see pass my circumstances.

I declare now that your wait is over. Your season is now. You have the power. You have the authority to bring your heart's desires to reality. Victory is yours. You will live debt-free with riches coming your way. Your words will speak positive things into your life, and your soul will prosper. Everything you touch shall prosper. Listen to God's Word, add your ingredient of faith, and go!

About the Author

Gary Hawkins, Sr. is a graduate of Luther Rice Seminary in Lithonia, Georgia. He is the founding pastor of Voices of Faith Ministries in Stone Mountain and Conyers, Georgia. Voices of Faith has seen its membership grow from 75 people to more than 9,000 in only seven years. It has been recognized by Church Growth Magazine as the 25th fastest growing church in America. Gary Hawkins, Sr. was recognized by The Church Report magazine as one of the top twenty-five leaders to watch in 2005 and listed in Strathmore's Who's Who in September 2006. Gary and his wife, Debbie, live in Loganville, Georgia with their four children, Elaina, Ashley, Gary Jr., and Kalen.

ORDER FORM
Order by phone, fax, mail, or online

Gary Hawkins Ministries
P. O. Box 870989
Stone Mountain, GA 30087

Phone: 770-498-5850
Fax: 770-498-1566
www.voicesfaith.org

QTY	ITEM	EACH	TOTAL
	Marketing Your Church for Growth – Book	$ 12.95	
	Marketing Your Church for Growth – Audio Cassette	10.95	
	Marketing Your Church for Growth – CD	15.95	
	Fighting for Your Destiny – Book	13.95	
	God's Best for Your Life	15.95	
	Marketing Through Faith – Home Work Study	50.00	
	Eight Steps to Prosperity	15.95	
	What Every Pastor Should Know	14.95	
	Marketing for Next Level Ministry – Book	15.95	
	From the Heart of First Ladies	15.95	
	What Every First Lady Should Know	14.95	
	COMING SOON:		
	The Scene Stealer	12.95	
	Marketing for the Next Dimension	15.95	
	Subtotal		$
	Postage and Handling (Call for Shipping Charges)		$
	Total		$

Name _____ Date _____

Address _____ Apt./Unit _____

City_____ State_____Zip _____

Payment Method: ☐ VISA ☐ MC ☐ AMEX ☐ Discover ☐ Check

Credit Card #_____ Exp. _____

Signature _____